# Mommy and Daddy want to F%#&

By

Michael Glouberman

Illustrated by

Dan Madia

It's Sunday morning
and dawn is breaking,
Daddy wakes
with something aching.

He turns to Mommy
With a hopeful smile
She's more than willing –
It's been a while.

The bed is noisy,
squeaky, risky
But they're in the mood
and feeling frisky.


So pillows and blankets
go on the floor…
But it's too late now –
they're at the door!

Good morning, children!
You are the best!
We have no doubt
We're heaven-blessed.


But can you give us
just ten minutes
So we can finish
Up some business?

It's complicated,
and we're ill at ease
To try explaining
the birds and bees.

It's just that you're
a little young
For where Daddy wants
to put his tongue.

You see, when a father
and a mother
Really, really
love each other

They have a need
an urge, a twitch
For something that
can scratch that itch!

So find a doll,
a book, a puzzle,
Just long enough
for us to nuzzle.


Your talking kitty,
or that cool T. Rex
Cuz Mommy and Daddy
need to have sex!

So have a snack,
eat what you please.
Mix some chocolate milk
with cheese.

Use the oven,
or toast some bread.
Doesn't Daddy deserve
a little head?

Do anything
your little hearts desire.
Go play with matches!
Start a fire!


Because all we need
is half an hour
To bump some uglies
in the shower.

Try juggling knives,
or take the car keys.
Catch some squirrels,
learn Congolese.


Go find your favorite
hiding place
So Mommy can sit on
Daddy's face.

Go play hopscotch,
jump some rope.
Anything that
gives us hope

That with the tiniest
bit of luck,
Mommy and Daddy
will get to f%#&!

It's called making love,
you little cuties!
To do the nasty,
Or bump some booties!
To hokey pokey
or fornicate
To get the runners
past home plate!
To BOFF!
To BANG!
To go balls deep!
To make the
angry weasel weep!

To DIDDLE!
BOINK!
Hide the salami!
Put part of Daddy
inside of Mommy!
To lay some pipe!
Butter the muffin!
Give the turkey
a little stuffin'!
Bash the beaver!
Smuggle the pickle!
Enjoy a little
slap and tickle!

Think like this,
try to imagine
That Daddy's got
a one-eyed dragon.


It can't relax,
calm down, behave
Until it hides
in Mommy's cave.

How about a nap?
Or just a snooze?
Cuz Daddy needs
to get some cooze.


And Mommy,
feeling quite fertile
Is in the mood
for doggy-style.

Go to the yard,
dig up some bugs.
Play on the roof,
or take some drugs.


Draw some pictures
you can bring us,
So we can practice
cunnilingus.

We're sorry if
we're angry-sounding.
But Mommy's hot
and needs a pounding.


So go away!
Leave us alone!
Mommy and Daddy
want to bone!

It's Sunday night,
the sun's gone deep.
The children are
at last asleep.

We're finally free
from being accosted…
But Mom's head hurts
and Dad's exhausted.

So they crawl back
underneath their covers,
Remembering days
when they were lovers.


Promising each other
that with some luck…
Someday soon
they'll get to f%#&.

26669076R00023

Made in the USA
Middletown, DE
03 December 2015